Greg —

See you At the top!

Terry

TO

_____

FROM

_____

INSPIRATION
from the Top

ZIG ZIGLAR

THOMAS NELSON
Since 1798

NASHVILLE   DALLAS   MEXICO CITY   RIO DE JANEIRO

It's not what you know or who you know.

It's what you are that finally counts.

ZIG ZIGLAR

Reading has been the fuel of my motivation. It has changed the direction in which I have traveled, and it has enhanced my creative imagination more than any other activity I have ever pursued. I'm now in my eighth decade of living, and I still read several hours a day. Why? When I can connect old information with new information, the combination of the two creates perspectives that could never have been achieved otherwise. New information makes new and fresh ideas possible.

I read for the *aha* moments, the information that makes a light bulb go off in my head. I want to put information in my mind that will be the most beneficial to me, my family, and my fellow man, financially, morally, spiritually, and emotionally. I seldom read anything that is not of a factual nature because I want to invest my time wisely in the things that will improve my life. Don't misunderstand: there is nothing wrong with reading purely for the joy of it. Novels have their place, but biographies of famous men and women contain information that can change lives. Dr. Norman Vincent Peale's *The Power of Positive Thinking* changed my thought processes. The Bible changed my believing. Ultimately, what I have read has changed my being.

If the *aha!* I get when I'm reading is not already reduced into one or two sentences, I'll take the essence of what I've read and chunk it into easily remembered bites of information. That information is what becomes "quotable." You would not sit still for me to read to you every book I've ever read. But if you're the least bit like me, you'll jump at the chance to bypass all the churning and scoop the cream right off the top. That is what quotes are—the cream of our learning.

The highest point
of achievement yesterday
is the starting point of today.

MOTTO OF PAULIST FATHERS

The right quote can inspire people to change their ways. I love to quote my mother: "Tell the truth and tell it ever, costeth what it will; for he who hides the wrong he did, does the wrong thing still." Of course, this quote didn't begin with my mother, but she is the first person who said it to me. Quotes, *good quotes*, are like that—you remember who said it, what the circumstances were, and that it had an immediate impact on your thinking.

I've compiled the quotes in this book with great care. I've included quotes that will help you on the work front, the home front, and the spiritual front. There are quotes to lift you up and quotes to bring you back to earth. Some will make you smile, and some will create more questions than you might care to think about. All of them will make you think, and that is an exercise that will enhance and improve your future immensely.

It is my hope that you "get" the same *aha*s I got when I first read or wrote the quotes I've selected for this inspirational book.

If you apply what you learn to your life, I can honestly say that I will see you at the top!

Zig Ziglar

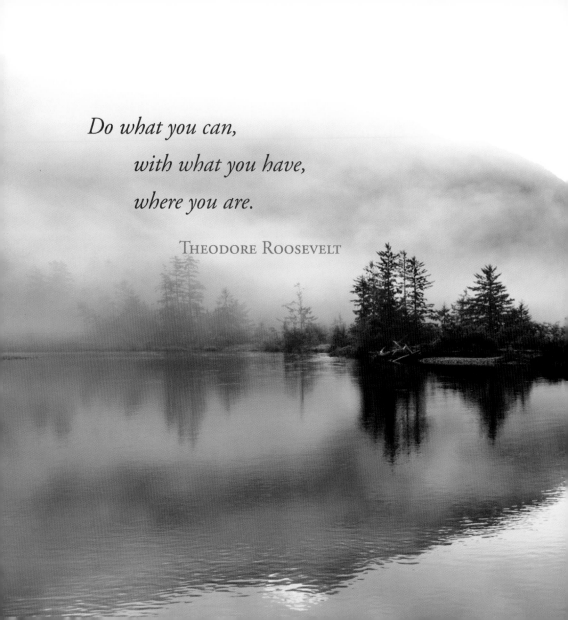

Do what you can,

with what you have,

where you are.

THEODORE ROOSEVELT

There is a wisdom of the head,
and . . .
there is a wisdom of the heart.

Charles Dickens

Faith believes

in spite of the circumstances

and acts in spite of the consequences.

ADRIAN ROGERS

Men are anxious to improve their circumstances,
but are unwilling to improve themselves;
they therefore remain bound.

James Allen

If your actions
inspire others
to dream more,

LEARN MORE,

do more,
and become more,
you are a leader.

JOHN QUINCY ADAMS

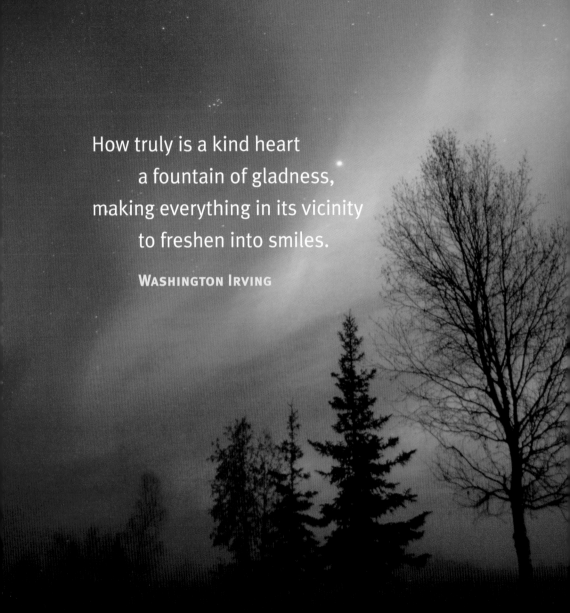

How truly is a kind heart
      a fountain of gladness,
making everything in its vicinity
      to freshen into smiles.

WASHINGTON IRVING

"FOR I KNOW THE PLANS I HAVE FOR YOU,"
DECLARES THE LORD, "PLANS TO PROSPER YOU
AND NOT TO HARM YOU,
PLANS TO GIVE YOU HOPE AND A FUTURE."
JEREMIAH 29:11

When joy and prayer are married,
their first born child is gratitude.

CHARLES SPURGEON

Forgiveness is the key that unlocks the door
of resentment and the handcuffs of hate.

William Arthur Ward

*I would maintain that thanks
is the highest form of thought;
and that gratitude is happiness doubled by wonder.*

G. K. CHESTERTON

Love from the center of who you are. . . .
Hold on for dear life to good.

ROMANS 12:9 MSG

The pleasantest things in the world are pleasant thoughts,
and the great art of life is to have as many of them as possible.

MICHEL DE MONTAIGNE

A HUMAN BEING CAN ALTER THEIR LIFE
BY ALTERING THEIR ATTITUDE. | WILLIAM JAMES

Great minds have purposes; others have wishes.

Washington Irving

"You can pray for anything,
and if you believe that you've received it,
it will be yours."

MARK 11:24 NLT

Never tell people how to do things.
Tell them what to do
and they will surprise you
with their ingenuity.

GENERAL GEORGE S. PATTON

*Most people who fail in their dreams
fail not from lack of ability
but from lack of commitment.*

Zig Ziglar

When you have a choice and don't make it,
that is in itself a choice.   WILLIAM JAMES

*Do nothing
out of selfish ambition
or vain conceit,*
BUT IN HUMILITY
consider others
better than yourself.

PHILIPPIANS 2:3

Adversity is the first path to truth.

LORD BYRON

A LOVING HEART IS THE TRUEST WISDOM.

CHARLES DICKENS

Don't be afraid to take a big step if needed.
You can't cross a chasm in two small jumps.

AUTHOR UNKNOWN

Actions are seeds of fate. Seeds grow into destiny.

Harry S. Truman

Every great dream

begins with a dreamer.

Always remember,

you have within you the strength,

the patience, and the passion

to reach for the stars to change the world.

HARRIET TUBMAN

*The more a man **knows**,*
*the more he **forgives**.*

Catherine the Great

Example is not the main thing
in influencing others.
It is the only thing.

ALBERT SCHWEITZER

It is neither wealth nor splendor,
but tranquility and occupation,
which give happiness.

THOMAS JEFFERSON

When you do the things you need to do
when you need to do them,
the day will come
when you can do the things
you want to do when you want to do them.

ZIG ZIGLAR

The LORD your God…
goes with you,
TO FIGHT FOR YOU
against your enemies,
to save you.

DEUTERONOMY 20:4 NKJV

*Every crucial experience
can be regarded as a setback—
or the start of a
new kind of development.*

MARY ROBERTS RINEHART

The future belongs to those
who believe in the beauty of their dreams.
ELEANOR ROOSEVELT

Input influences outlook,
outlook influences output,
and output determines outcome.
AUTHOR UNKNOWN

All that we love deeply
becomes a part of us.
HELEN KELLER

Each of us will one day be judged
by our standard of life,
not by our standard of living;
by our measure of giving,
not by our measure of wealth;
by our simple goodness,
not by our seeming greatness.

WILLIAM ARTHUR WARD

Until you commit your goals to paper,
you have intentions that are seeds without soil.

AUTHOR UNKNOWN

As iron sharpens iron, so a friend sharpens a friend.

Proverbs 27:17 NLT

Be substantially great in thyself,
and more than thou appearest unto others.

SIR THOMAS BROWNE

The deepest principle in human nature
is the craving to be appreciated. William James

If you aren't fired with enthusiasm,
you will be fired with enthusiasm.

Vince Lombardi

Keep your lives free
from the love of money
and be content
with what you have.

Hebrews 13:5

People spend their lives
in the service of their passions
instead of employing their passions
in the service of their lives.

SIR RICHARD STEELE

PEOPLE WILL NOT BEAR IT WHEN ADVICE IS VIOLENTLY GIVEN,
EVEN IF IT IS WELL FOUNDED. HEARTS ARE FLOWERS;
THEY REMAIN OPEN TO THE SOFTLY FALLING DEW,
BUT SHUT UP IN THE VIOLENT DOWNPOUR OF RAIN.

JOHN PAUL RICHTER

Evidence is conclusive that your self-talk
has a direct bearing on your performance.

ZIG ZIGLAR

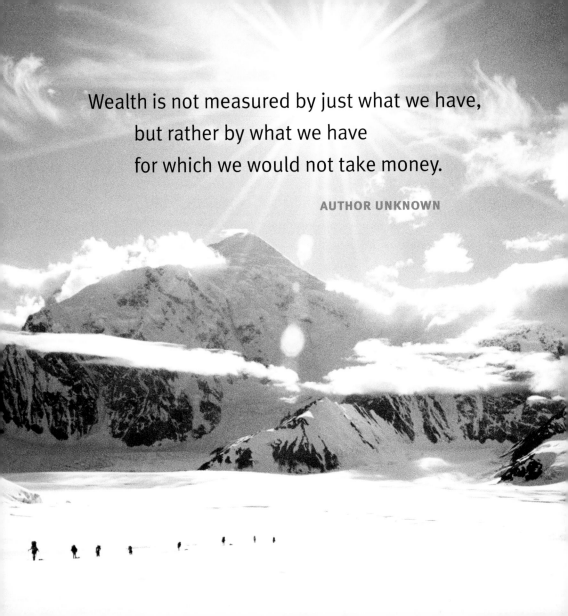

Wealth is not measured by just what we have,
but rather by what we have
for which we would not take money.

AUTHOR UNKNOWN

No one can make you feel inferior
without your consent.
Eleanor Roosevelt

Winning is not a sometime thing; it's an all-the-time thing.

VINCE LOMBARDI

Reputation is what men think of us;
character is what God
and angels know of us.

THOMAS PAINE

In the middle of every difficulty
comes opportunity.

ALBERT EINSTEIN

The happiness of most people we know
is not ruined by
great catastrophes or fatal errors,
but by the repetition
of slowly destructive little things.

ERNEST DIMNET

Seek to do good and you will find that happiness will run after you.

JAMES FREEMAN CLARKE

You will become as small
as your controlling desire,
as great as your dominant aspiration.

JAMES ALLEN

"This is the very best way to love. Put your life on the line for your friends."
JOHN 15:13 MSG

The only thing we have to fear
IS FEAR ITSELF.

FRANKLIN DELANO ROOSEVELT

*The most important thing about goals is . . .
having one.*

GEOFFREY F. ABERT

———————

Whatever I have tried to do in life,
I have tried with all my heart to do well;
that whatever I have devoted myself to,
I have devoted myself to completely;
that in great aims and in small,
I have always been thoroughly in earnest.

CHARLES DICKENS

Who has not served cannot command.

JOHN FLORIO

Success Procedure:

Run your day by the clock and your life with a vision.

Zig Ziglar

Always do more than is required of you.

GENERAL GEORGE S. PATTON

Even if you're on the right track,
you'll get run over if you just sit there.

Will Rogers

In your hands you hold the seeds of failure
or the potential for greatness.
Your hands are capable,
but they must be used and for the right things
to reap the rewards you are capable of attaining.
The choice is yours.

ZIG ZIGLAR

Rejoice in the Lord,

    and your bones will flourish . . .

    and your cheeks will glow. . . .

Joy is balm and healing,

    and if you will but rejoice,

    God will give power.

A. B. Simpson

THE SUPREME ACCOMPLISHMENT IS TO BLUR
THE LINE BETWEEN WORK AND PLAY.

ARNOLD TOYNBEE

Self-respect *is the fruit of discipline.*

ABRAHAM J. HESCHEL

Where there is no vision,
the people perish.

PROVERBS 29:18 KJV

You know you are old

when you have lost all your marvels.

MERRY BROWNE

Defeat should never be
a source of discouragement,
but rather a fresh stimulus.

BISHOP ROBERT SOUTH

**Be strong and do not give up,
for your work will be rewarded.**

2 CHRONICLES 15:7

Your greatness is measured
by your horizons.

MICHELANGELO

Men are governed only by serving them;
the rule is without exception.

Victor Cousin

Four short words sum up what lifted
        most successful individuals above the crowd:
A LITTLE BIT MORE.
They did all that was expected of them and . . .
        a little bit more. | A. LOU VICKERY

The biggest tragedy in America

is not the great waste of natural resources—
though this is tragic;

the biggest tragedy is

the waste of human resources
because the average person
goes to his grave with his music still in him.

Oliver Wendell Holmes

Optimism is

THE FAITH THAT LEADS

TO ACHIEVEMENT.

Nothing can be done

WITHOUT HOPE

and confidence.

HELEN KELLER

In this world a man must either be

an anvil or a hammer.

Henry Wadsworth Longfellow

A person is not defeated by their opponents

but by themselves.

Jan Christiaan Smuts

Genius is 1 percent inspiration
and 99 percent perspiration.

Thomas A. Edison

CHARACTER
is what you are in the dark.

D. L. MOODY

COMMIT YOUR WAY TO THE LORD;
TRUST IN HIM AND HE WILL DO THIS.

PSALM 37:5

Real optimism is aware of problems
BUT RECOGNIZES SOLUTIONS;
knows about difficulties
but believes they can be overcome;
sees the negatives
BUT ACCENTUATES THE POSITIVES;
is exposed to the worst but expects the best;
has reason to complain
but chooses to smile.

WILLIAM ARTHUR WARD

BLIND ZEAL IS SOON PUT TO A SHAMEFUL RETREAT,
WHILE HOLY RESOLUTION, BUILT ON FAST PRINCIPLES,
LIFTS UP ITS HEAD LIKE A ROCK IN THE MIDST OF THE WAVES.

WILLIAM GURNALL

The true wisdom is
    to be always seasonable,
    and to change with a good grace
in changing circumstances.

Robert Louis Stevenson

I never think of the future. It comes soon enough.

Albert Einstein

The doors

OF WISDOM

are never shut.

BENJAMIN FRANKLIN

An optimist is someone who believes

that a house fly is looking

for a way to get out.

GEORGE GENE NATHAN

Character is not in the mind;

it is in the will.

Fulton J. Sheen

The most important opinion
is the one you have of yourself,
and the most significant
things you say all day
are those things you say to yourself.

Zig Ziglar

WE MAKE A LIVING BY WHAT WE GET,
BUT WE MAKE A LIFE BY WHAT WE GIVE.

WINSTON CHURCHILL

The world is moving so fast these days
that the person who says it can't be done
is generally interrupted by someone doing it.

ELBERT HUBBARD

If you do not hope,

you will not find what is beyond your hopes.

St. Clement of Alexandria

MOTIV

is the spark that lights the fire

OF KNOWLEDGE

ATION

AND FUELS THE ENGINE OF ACCOMPLISHMENT. *It maximizes and maintains* MOMENTUM.

ZIG ZIGLAR

Men's best successes come after their disappointments.

HENRY WARD BEECHER

Blessed are those who dream dreams
and are willing to pay the price
to make them come true.

HENRY VISCARDI JR.

Success means having the courage,
the determination, and the will to become the person
you believe you were meant to be.

GEORGE SHEEHAN

The way you see your future
determines
your thinking today.
YOUR THINKING TODAY
DETERMINES
YOUR PERFORMANCE TODAY.
Your performance in the todays
of your life
determines your future.

ZIG ZIGLAR

When dads shoot straight,

the kids will hit the mark.

Adrian Rogers

We shall never know all the good
that a simple smile can do.

MOTHER TERESA

OUR WORDS REVEAL OUR THOUGHTS;

MANNERS MIRROR OUR SELF-ESTEEM;

OUR ACTIONS REFLECT OUR CHARACTER;

OUR HABITS PREDICT THE FUTURE.

William Arthur Ward

WHEN YOUR GOALS

ARE CLEARLY DEFINED

AND INTELLIGENTLY SET,

YOU HAVE, IN ESSENCE,

TAKEN A MAJOR STEP TOWARD

PROGRAMMING YOUR LEFT BRAIN.

THAT FREES YOUR RIGHT BRAIN

TO BE ITS CREATIVE BEST.

ZIG ZIGLAR

Nothing in this world can take the place of persistence.

Talent will not; nothing is more common

than unsuccessful people with talent.

Genius will not; unrewarded genius is almost a proverb.

Education will not; the world is full of educated derelicts.

Persistence and determination alone are omnipotent.

CALVIN COOLIDGE

Be joyful in hope, patient in affliction,
faithful in prayer.

ROMANS **12:12**

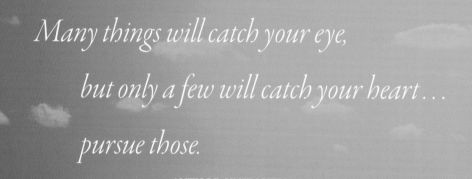

Many things will catch your eye,

but only a few will catch your heart…

pursue those.

AUTHOR UNKNOWN

What counts is not necessarily
the size of the dog in the fight—
it's the size of the fight in the dog.

DWIGHT D. EISENHOWER

You don't have to be great to start, but you have to start to be great.

JOE SABAH

If you judge people,

you don't have time to love them.

Mother Teresa

MOST AMERICANS
honestly believe America is the most powerful nation on earth, BUT ACTUALLY the most powerful nation is *imagi*-nation.

ZIG ZIGLAR

The U.S. Constitution
doesn't guarantee happiness,
only the pursuit of it.
You have to catch up with it yourself.

Benjamin Franklin

Success is not measured by what a person accomplishes,
but by the opposition they have encountered,
and the courage with which
they have maintained the struggle
against overwhelming odds.

ORISON SWETT MARDEN

KIDS DON'T MAKE UP

100 percent of our population,

but they do make up

100 percent of our future.

ZIG ZIGLAR

There are two ways of spreading light:
to be the candle
or the mirror that reflects it.

EDITH WHARTON

FRIENDSHIP IS THE ONLY CEMENT
THAT WILL EVER HOLD THE WORLD TOGETHER.

Woodrow Wilson

Not in the clamor of the crowded street,

nor in the shouts and plaudits of the throng,

but in ourselves are triumph and defeat.

Henry Wadsworth Longfellow

Take calculated risks.
That is quite different from being rash.
GENERAL GEORGE S. PATTON

Failure is an event, not a person.
So regardless of what happens to you along the way,
*   you must keep on going and doing*
*   the right thing in the right way.*
Then the event becomes a reality of a changed life.

Zig Ziglar

Do not wish to be anything
but what you are,
and try to be that perfectly.

St. Francis de Sales

I learned a great many new words that day.
I do not remember what they all were,
but I do know that mother, father, sister,
teacher *were among them —*
words that were to make the world blossom
for me "like Aaron's rod, with flowers."
It would have been difficult to find
a happier child than I was as I lay in my bed
at the close of that eventful day
and lived over the joys it had brought me,
and for the first time longed
for a new day to come.

HELEN KELLER

IF YOU ARE
WEARING OUT THE SEAT
OF YOUR PANTS
*before you
do your shoe soles,*
you are making
too many contacts
in the wrong place.

AUTHOR UNKNOWN

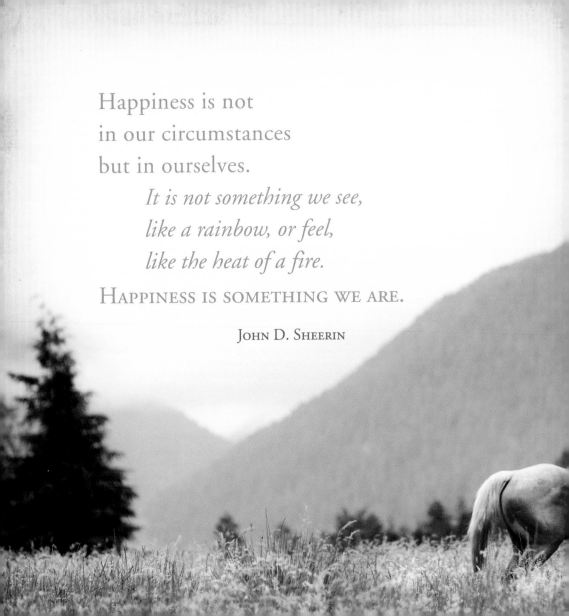

Happiness is not
in our circumstances
but in ourselves.

It is not something we see,
like a rainbow, or feel,
like the heat of a fire.

HAPPINESS IS SOMETHING WE ARE.

JOHN D. SHEERIN

It is better to be divided by truth than to be united by error.

Adrian Rogers

Some people think they have burning ambition when it is merely inflammation of the wishbone.

WILLIAM JAMES

EACH DAY COMES BEARING ITS OWN GIFTS.
UNTIE THE RIBBONS.

RUTH ANN SCHABACKER

By nature we have no defect that could not become a strength,
no strength that could not become a defect.

JOHANN WOLFGANG VON GOETHE

The greatest good we can do for anyone

is not to share our wealth with them,

but rather to reveal their own wealth to them.

It's astonishing how much talent and ability rests

inside a human being.

Zig Ziglar

It is hard to fail,
but it is worse never
to have tried to succeed.
THEODORE ROOSEVELT

Too often, the opportunity knocks,
but by the time you disengage the chain,
push back the bolt, unhook the two locks,
and shut off the burglar alarms, it's too late.

RITA COOLIDGE

Some people drink at the fountain of knowledge.
Others just gargle.

AUTHOR UNKNOWN

Reading makes a man full.

Francis Bacon

It is easy to dodge
OUR RESPONSIBILITIES,
but we cannot dodge
the consequences
of dodging our
responsibilities.

SIR JOSIAH STAMP

People were designed for accomplishment, engineered for success,

DESIGNED

and endowed with the seeds of greatness.

ZIG ZIGLAR

FOR GREATNESS

When you clearly understand

that success is a process, not an event,

you are encouraged to follow the right process

to create the success you are capable of having.

ZIG ZIGLAR

An investment in knowledge pays the best interest.

Benjamin Franklin

If you have a tendency to brag,
just remember it's not the whistle
that pulls the train.

O. F. NICHOLS

Quality is never an accident.
It is always the result of intelligent effort.

John Ruskin

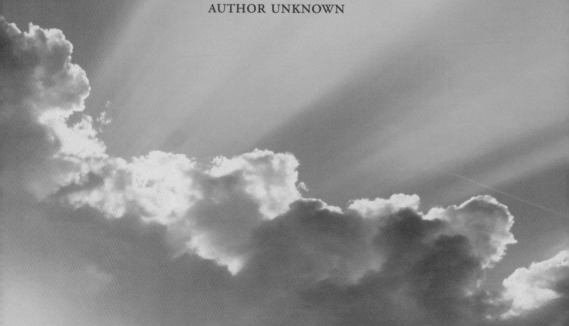

*Grandmother/grandchild
relationships are simple:
grandmas are short on criticism and long on love.*

AUTHOR UNKNOWN

Happiness is not a when or a where;
it can be a here and a now.
But until you are happy with who you are
you will never be happy
because of what you have.

Zig Ziglar

Weakness of attitude
becomes weakness of character.

Albert Einstein

The greatest use
OF LIFE
is to spend it
FOR SOMETHING
THAT WILL
outlast it.

WILLIAM JAMES

We are always in the forge, or on the anvil;

by trials God is shaping us for higher things.

HENRY WARD BEECHER

You might not be
what you say you are,
but what you say,
you are. | ZIG ZIGLAR

HE CLIMBS HIGHEST WHO HELPS ANOTHER UP.

GEORGE MATTHEW ADAMS

Husbands, if you treat your wife
    like a thoroughbred, chances are good
    you won't end up with a nag.
Wives, if you treat your husband
    like a champ, chances are even better
    that you won't end up with a chump.

ZIG ZIGLAR

All we need to make us really happy
is something to be enthusiastic about.

Charles Kingsley

A journey of a thousand miles begins with a single step.
CHINESE PROVERB

Adversity causes some people to break,

others to break records.

William Arthur Ward

But as for you, be strong and do not give up,
for your work will be rewarded.

2 CHRONICLES 15:7

The future is as bright as the promises of God.

ADONIRAM JUDSON

Recognizing a problem

or weakness

is the first step

in remedying it.

DONALD LAIRA

Have you had a kindness shown?
Pass it on. . . .
Let it travel down the years,
let it wipe another's tears,
till in heaven the deed appears.
Pass it on. | Henry Burton

Watch your thoughts; they become words.

Watch your words; they become actions.

Watch your actions; they become habits.

Watch your habits; they become character.

Watch your character; it becomes your destiny.

Frank Outlaw

Well done is better than well said.

Benjamin Franklin

Never be haughty to the humble;

never be humble to the haughty.

JEFFERSON DAVIS

*Though no one can go back
and make a brand-new start,
anyone can start from now
and make a brand-new ending.*

CARL BARD

The truth is,
fear and immorality
are two of the greatest
inhibitors of performance.

ZIG ZIGLAR

Pleasure is very seldom found where it is sought.
Our brightest blazes are commonly
kindled by unexpected sparks.

SAMUEL JOHNSON

THE PRICE OF GREATNESS IS RESPONSIBILITY.

WINSTON CHURCHILL

When the heart
is full of joy,
IT ALLOWS
its joy to escape. . . .
The full heart is
THE OVERFLOWING
heart.

CHARLES SPURGEON

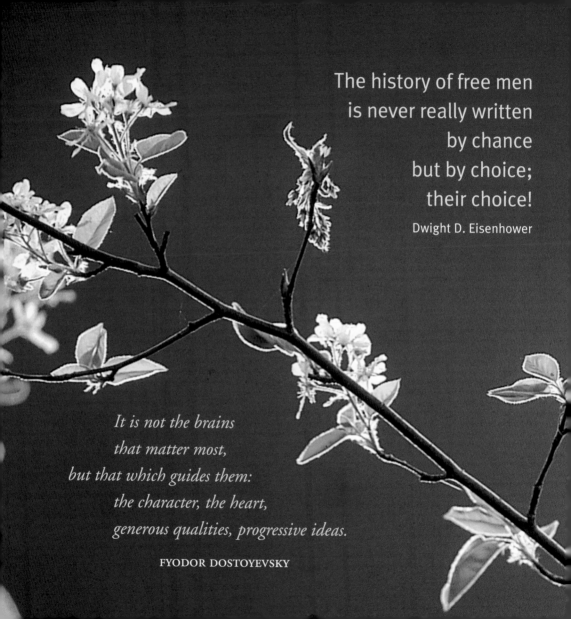

The history of free men
is never really written
by chance
but by choice;
their choice!

Dwight D. Eisenhower

It is not the brains
that matter most,
but that which guides them:
the character, the heart,
generous qualities, progressive ideas.

FYODOR DOSTOYEVSKY

**Do not pray for tasks
equal to your powers;**

pray for powers equal to your tasks.

PHILLIPS BROOKS

When the going gets tough,
those with a dream keep going.

BEN FELDMAN

In our country you are free to choose,
but the choices you make today
will determine what you will be, do,
and have in the tomorrows of your life.

Zig Ziglar

No horse gets anywhere until he is harnessed.
No stream or gas drives anything until it is confined. . . .
No life ever grows great until it is focused,
dedicated, and disciplined.

HARRY EMERSON FOSDICK

Work with

ENTHUSIASM,
*as though
you were working*
FOR THE LORD
rather than for people.

EPHESIANS 6:7 NLT

Grandchildren are God's way

of compensating us for growing old.

Mary H. Waldripa

What you get by achieving your goals
is not as important as what
you become by achieving your goals. | Zig Ziglar

A person hears only what they understand.

JOHANN WOLFGANG VON GOETHE

Let me win,

but if I cannot win,

let me be brave in the attempt.

MOTTO OF THE SPECIAL OLYMPICS

A strong passion for any object will ensure success,

for the desire of the end will point out the means.

WILLIAM HAZLITT

A pleasing personality
	helps you win friends and influence people.
Add character to that formula,
	and you keep those friends
	and maintain the influence.

ZIG ZIGLAR

YOU LEARN TO LOVE BY LOVING.

St. Francis de Sales

Security comes from your ability to produce.

In short, it is an inside job.

GENERAL DOUGLAS MACARTHUR

WE CAN DO NO GREAT THINGS—

ONLY SMALL THINGS WITH GREAT LOVE.

MOTHER TERESA

WE ALL FIND TIME
to do what
we really want to do.

WILLIAM FEATHER

It is pleasing to God whenever you rejoice
or laugh from the bottom of your heart.

MARTIN LUTHER

What a man knows
only through feeling
can be explained
only through enthusiasm.

JOSEPH JOUBERT

You can have everything in life you want

if you will just help enough other people

get what they want. | **ZIG ZIGLAR**

One learns people through the heart,

not the eyes or the intellect.

Mark Twain

WITHOUT HOPE,
PEOPLE ARE ONLY HALF ALIVE.
WITH HOPE, THEY DREAM AND THINK AND WORK.

CHARLES SAWYER

You can have total success when you
balance your physical, mental, and spiritual as well as
your personal, family, and business life.

ZIG ZIGLAR

CHARACTER

is the total of thousands of small daily strivings

to live up to the best that is in us.

LIEUTENANT GENERAL ARTHUR TRUDEAU

THE SECRET OF HAPPINESS
IS TO ADMIRE
WITHOUT DESIRING.

F. H. Bradley

Perfection exists not in doing
extraordinary things
but in doing ordinary things
extraordinarily well.
ANGELIQUE ARNAULD

PROGRESS INVOLVES RISKS.
YOU CAN'T STEAL SECOND BASE
AND KEEP YOUR FOOT ON FIRST.

Frederick B. Wilcox

A wise man will make more opportunities
than he finds. | FRANCIS BACON

Stay within whispering distance.
If you stray,
you won't hear His voice.

AUTHOR UNKNOWN

A goal casually set and lightly taken
is freely abandoned at the first obstacle.

ZIG ZIGLAR

OPPORTUNITY MAY KNOCK ONCE,
BUT TEMPTATION BANGS ON YOUR FRONT DOOR FOREVER.

AUTHOR UNKNOWN

Obstacles are
those frightful things you see
**when you take your eyes
off your goals.**

Sydney Smith

T A L

We deny our talents
and abilities

because to acknowlege or confess them

E N T

WOULD COMMIT US TO USE THEM.

ZIG ZIGLAR

I WILL PREPARE MYSELF
AND SOME DAY
MY CHANCE WILL COME.

Abraham Lincoln

Eyes that look are common; eyes that see are rare.

J. OSWALD SANDERS

Learning is not compulsory . . .

neither is survival.

W. EDWARDS DEMING

*Never lose sight
of the fact*
THAT THE MOST
important yardstick
OF YOUR SUCCESS
will be how
you treat other people.

BARBARA BUSH

The larger the island of knowledge,
the longer the shoreline of wonder.

RALPH W. STOCKMAN

I have never met an unhappy giver.

George Adams

You can't change the past,
but you can ruin a perfectly good present
by worrying about the future.

AUTHOR UNKNOWN

You have been given citizenship in a country like none other on earth, with opportunities available to you like nowhere else on earth. What will be asked of you is hard work; nothing will be handed to you. . . . Use your education and success in life to help those still trapped in cycles of poverty and violence. Above all, never lose faith in America. Its faults are yours to fix, not to curse.

GENERAL COLIN POWELL

If we truly love people,

WE WILL DESIRE FOR

THEM FAR MORE THAN

it is within our power

to give them,

and this will

LEAD US TO PRAYER.

RICHARD J. FOSTER

The bee is more honored than other animals,

not because she labors,

but because she labors for others.

St. John Chrysostom

LIFE IS NOT ABOUT WAITING FOR THE STORMS TO PASS . . .
IT'S ABOUT LEARNING HOW TO DANCE IN THE RAIN.

AUTHOR UNKNOWN

What I hear, I forget.
What I see, I remember.
What I do, I know.

CHINESE PROVERB

The mediocre teacher tells;
the good teacher explains;
the superior teacher demonstrates;
the great teacher inspires.

William Arthur Ward

OPPORTUNITIES ARE SELDOM LABELED.

CLAUDE McDONALD

God has given each of you a gift
from his great variety of spiritual gifts.
Use them well to serve one another.

1 PETER 4:10 NLT

Wisdom is knowledge
which has become a part of one's being.

ORRISON SWETT MARDEN

He that cannot forgive others
breaks the bridge
over which he,
himself,
must pass.

Lord Herbert

I bring you the gift of these four words:
I believe in you. | Blaise Pascal

SUCCESS IS OFTEN NOTHING MORE THAN
MOVING FROM ONE FAILURE TO THE NEXT
WITH UNDIMINISHED ENTHUSIASM.
Winston Churchill

The longer we follow the right path
the easier it becomes.
AUTHOR UNKNOWN

A good leader takes more than
their fair share of the blame
and gives more than their share of the credit.

ARNOLD GLASGOW

Man's mind, once stretched by a new idea,
never regains its original dimensions.

OLIVER WENDELL HOLMES

Win without boasting.

Lose without excuses.

Vince Lombardi

Whoever loves much does much.

Thomas à Kempis

IN THE END,
it's not the years in your life
THAT COUNT.
It's the life in your years.

ABRAHAM LINCOLN

A HOME IS A HOUSE
WITH A HEART INSIDE.

AUTHOR UNKNOWN

Your aspirations are your possibilities.

Samuel Johnson

THE QUALITY OF A PERSON'S LIFE IS IN DIRECT PROPORTION
TO THEIR COMMITMENT TO EXCELLENCE,
REGARDLESS OF THEIR CHOSEN FIELD OF ENDEAVOR.

VINCE LOMBARDI

A well-developed sense of humor
is the pole
that adds balance to your steps
as you walk the tightrope of life.

William Arthur Ward

A stumble may prevent a fall.

THOMAS FULLER

IF PASSION DRIVES YOU, LET REASON HOLD THE REINS.

Benjamin Franklin

A single idea can transform a person,

a life, a business, a nation, a world.

AUTHOR UNKNOWN

Chance favors the prepared mind.
LOUIS PASTEUR

Do you not know

    that those who run in a race all run,

    but one receives the prize?

Run in such a way that you may obtain it.

        1 CORINTHIANS 9:24 NKJV

I FOUND THAT
THE MEN AND WOMEN
who got to the top
were those that did the jobs
they had in hand
WITH EVERYTHING
they had of energy,
enthusiasm,
and hard work.

HARRY S. TRUMAN

FOLLOW HARD AFTER HIM,

and He will never fail you.

C. H. SPURGEON

People are like sticks of dynamite.
The power's on the inside,
but nothing happens
until the fuse gets lit.

MAC ANDERSON

The difference between

failure and success

is doing a thing

nearly right

and doing it

exactly right.

AUTHOR UNKNOWN

It is a funny thing about life;

if you refuse to accept anything but the best,

you very often get it.

W. Somerset Maugham

HAPPINESS IS A CHOICE, NOT A RESPONSE.

AUTHOR UNKNOWN

This one step—choosing a goal
and sticking to it—changes everything.

SCOTT REED

They who would accomplish little
must sacrifice little;
they who would achieve much
must sacrifice much.

JAMES ALLEN

Regardless of your lot in life,

YOU CAN

BUILD SOMETHING

BEAUTIFUL ON IT.

Zig Ziglar

You may have to
FIGHT A BATTLE
more than once to win it.

MARGARET THATCHER

PRAY, AND LET GOD WORRY.

Martin Luther

He who sows courtesy reaps friendship,

and he who plants kindness gathers love.

Saint Basil

THE MIRACLE, OR THE POWER, THAT ELEVATES THE FEW
IS TO BE FOUND IN THEIR INDUSTRY, APPLICATION,
AND PERSEVERANCE UNDER THE PROMPTING
OF A BRAVE, DETERMINED SPIRIT. | **MARK TWAIN**

The service we render others
is the rent we pay for our room on earth.

Wilfred Grenfell

Great works are performed

not by strength but by perseverance.

SAMUEL JOHNSON

The heart that gives . . .
gathers. | Hannah More

Never be lazy, but work hard
and serve the Lord enthusiastically.

ROMANS 12:11 NLT

Anyone can hold the helm

when the sea is calm.

PUBLILIUS SYRUS

A QUIET CONSCIENCE SLEEPS IN THUNDER.

ENGLISH PROVERB

Always bear in mind
that your own resolution to succeed
is more important
than any one thing.

Abraham Lincoln

*You seldom
come across anything*

more enjoyable

THAN A

HAPPY PERSON.

It is not the things we get,

but the hearts we touch,

that will measure our success in life.

AUTHOR UNKNOWN

It's the constant and determined effort

that breaks down all resistance,

sweeps away all obstacles.

CLAUDE M. BRISTOL

LIFE IS LIKE A GAME OF TENNIS;

THE PLAYER WHO SERVES WELL SELDOM LOSES.

AUTHOR UNKNOWN

Keep adding, keep walking, keep advancing;
do not stop, do not turn back,
do not turn from the straight road.

ST. AUGUSTINE

Money never made anyone rich.

SENECA

*God does not give us
everything we want,
but He does
fulfill His promises.*

DIETRICH BONHOEFFER

No one is useless

IN THIS WORLD
WHO LIGHTENS
THE BURDEN OF IT
to anyone else.

CHARLES DICKENS

COMMITMENT
is what transforms
a promise
to reality.

AUTHOR UNKNOWN

Courage is resistance to fear,
mastery of fear—
not absence of fear.

MARK TWAIN

Our ego is our silent partner—

too often with a controlling interest.

CULLEN HIGHTOWER

ANGER IS THE WIND
THAT BLOWS OUT THE LAMP OF THE MIND.

ROBERT G. INGERSOLL

The man on top of the mountain didn't fall there.
AUTHOR UNKNOWN

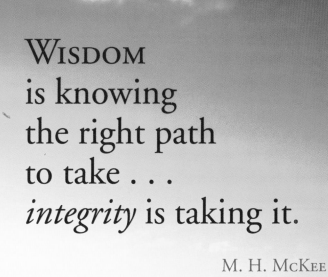

WISDOM
is knowing
the right path
to take . . .
integrity is taking it.

M. H. McKEE

Not in time, place,

or circumstances

but in the person lies success.

Charles B. Rouss

To get what we've never had,
we must do what we've never done.

AUTHOR UNKNOWN

All things work together for good
to those who love God,
to those who are the called
according to His purpose. | ROMANS 8:28 NKJV

THE BEGINNING OF A HABIT
is like an invisible thread,
but every time we repeat the act
we strengthen the strand,
add to it another filament,
until it becomes a great cable
that binds us irrevocably
through thought and act.

ORRISON SWETT MARDEN

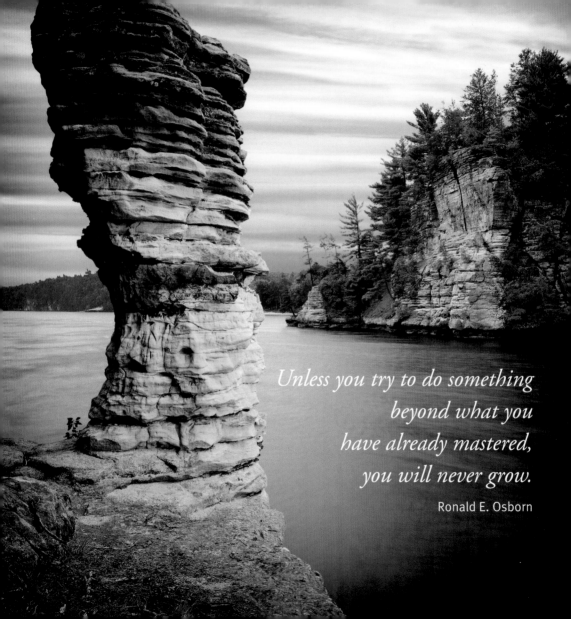

*Unless you try to do something
beyond what you
have already mastered,
you will never grow.*

Ronald E. Osborn

By perseverance the snail reached the ark.

C. H. Spurgeon

The young do not follow our preachings—

they follow us.

ROBERT BRAULT

Wherever you go . . .
go there with all your heart.

AUTHOR UNKNOWN

No person was ever honored

for what he received.

Honor has been the reward for what he gave.

CALVIN COOLIDGE

SUCCESS IS

THE MAXIMUM UTILIZATION

OF THE ABILITY

THAT YOU HAVE.

Zig Ziglar

Advice is like snow—
the softer it falls,
THE LONGER
IT DWELLS UPON,
and the deeper
IT SINKS
INTO THE MIND.

SAMUEL TAYLOR COLERIDGE

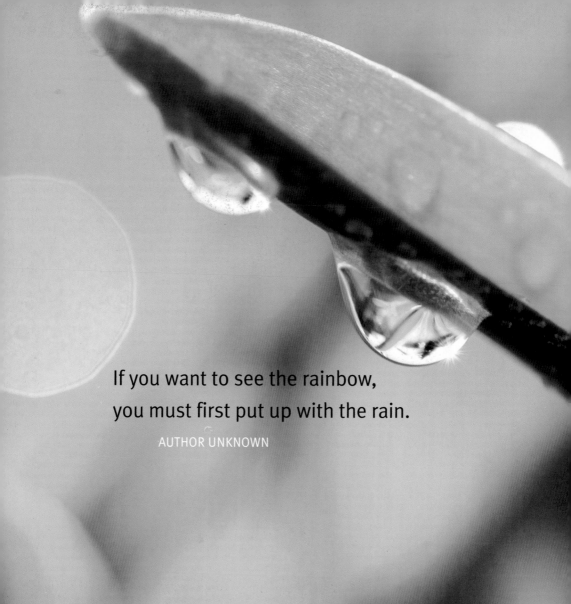

If you want to see the rainbow,
you must first put up with the rain.

AUTHOR UNKNOWN